T0012779

A **Books for a Better Earth**™ Title
The Books for a Better Earth™ collection is designed to inspire young people to become active, knowledgeable participants in caring for the planet they live on. Focusing on solutions to climate change challenges and human environmental impacts, the collection looks at how scientists, activists, and young leaders are working to safeguard Earth's future.

For Nathan and Kiley,
to quote Jane Goodall, "What you do makes a difference, and you
have to decide what kind of difference you want to make." —D.R.

For my children, Adele and Adriel, with all my love —Z.C.

ACKNOWLEDGMENTS
A big thank you to Kellie DuBay Gillis and Melody Von Smith for their time and expertise.
And all my gratitude to the wonderful librarians at the Library of Congress—
several sources were discovered with their research assistance!

Text copyright © 2023 by Deanna Romito
Illustrations copyright © 2023 by Holiday House Publishing, Inc.
All Rights Reserved
HOLIDAY HOUSE is registered in the U.S. Patent and Trademark Office.
Printed and bound in February 2024 at C&C Offset, Shenzhen, China.
The artwork was created with Procreate on iPad.
www.holidayhouse.com
First hardcover edition published in 2023
First paperback edition published in 2024
3 5 7 9 10 8 6 4 2

Library of Congress Cataloging-in-Publication Data

Names: Romito, Dee, author. | Chen, Ziyue, illustrator.
Title: The last plastic straw : a plastic problem and finding ways to fix it / by Dee Romito ; illustrated by Ziyue Chen.
Description: First edition. | New York : Holiday House, [2023] | Includes bibliographical references. | Audience: Ages 6–9
Audience: Grades 2–3 | Summary: "A history of the technological advancements behind the straw, how modern plastic straws harm the environment, and what is being done to solve the problem of plastic pollution" –Provided by publisher.
Identifiers: LCCN 2022008384 | ISBN 9780823449491 (hardcover)
Subjects: LCSH: Drinking straws–Juvenile literature. | Plastic scrap–Environmental aspects–Juvenile literature. | Disposable tableware–Environmental aspects–Juvenile literature. | Waste minimization–Juvenile literature.
Classification: LCC TD798 .R66 2023 | DDC 363.72/88–dc23/eng/20220407
LC record available at https://lccn.loc.gov/2022008384

ISBN: 978-0-8234-4949-1 (hardcover)
ISBN: 978-0-8234-5878-3 (paperback)

THE LAST PLASTIC STRAW

A PLASTIC PROBLEM AND FINDING WAYS TO FIX IT

BY
DEE ROMITO

ILLUSTRATED BY
ZIYUE CHEN

books for a better earth™

holiday house • new york

Over five thousand years ago, the ancient Sumerians had a problem.

They needed a way to avoid the icky substances in their beverages. The barley-based drink they brewed was thick, and the undrinkable solids sunk to the bottom.

Luckily, the people of Sumer were a problem-solving kind of civilization. They were the first to create a system of writing, the plow, sailboats, and even the wheel!

Their solution was to use a reed—a hollow grass that made it easy to sip the liquid directly from the top of the drink. However, royals like Queen Puabi, the Sumerian Queen of Ur, drank from long, gold tubes with precious blue stone inside.

These are the earliest known drinking straws. The clues to their history were found in Queen Puabi's royal tomb!

QUEEN PUABI

Over the thousands of years that followed, drinking tubes showed up in other areas of the world too. In China, they used plant stalks to drink wine. In South America, they used a silver or bronze "bombilla" with a filter on the end to drink tea.

In the 1800s, people used rye stalks for straws, but there was a bit of a problem.

The rye left a gritty residue which changed the taste of the drink, and it broke down in the liquid. People literally used "straw" or dried stalks of grain to drink. *That's* why we call them straws!

On a hot day in Washington, DC, Marvin Stone was drinking a popular drink called a mint julep. But he'd had enough of that grassy taste from the rye stalk.

Marvin took a pencil, wrapped paper around it, slipped the pencil out, and used glue to hold the paper together. The modern drinking straw was born!

He later added a wax coating so the straw wouldn't break down from the liquids.

MARVIN STONE

Marvin patented the design for the "Artificial Straw" in 1888, which means he filed it with the government so only he could produce his invention. He formed a company and invented a machine to roll the straws. Soon his factory was producing two million straws per day!

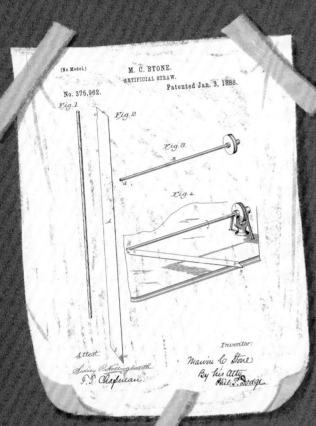

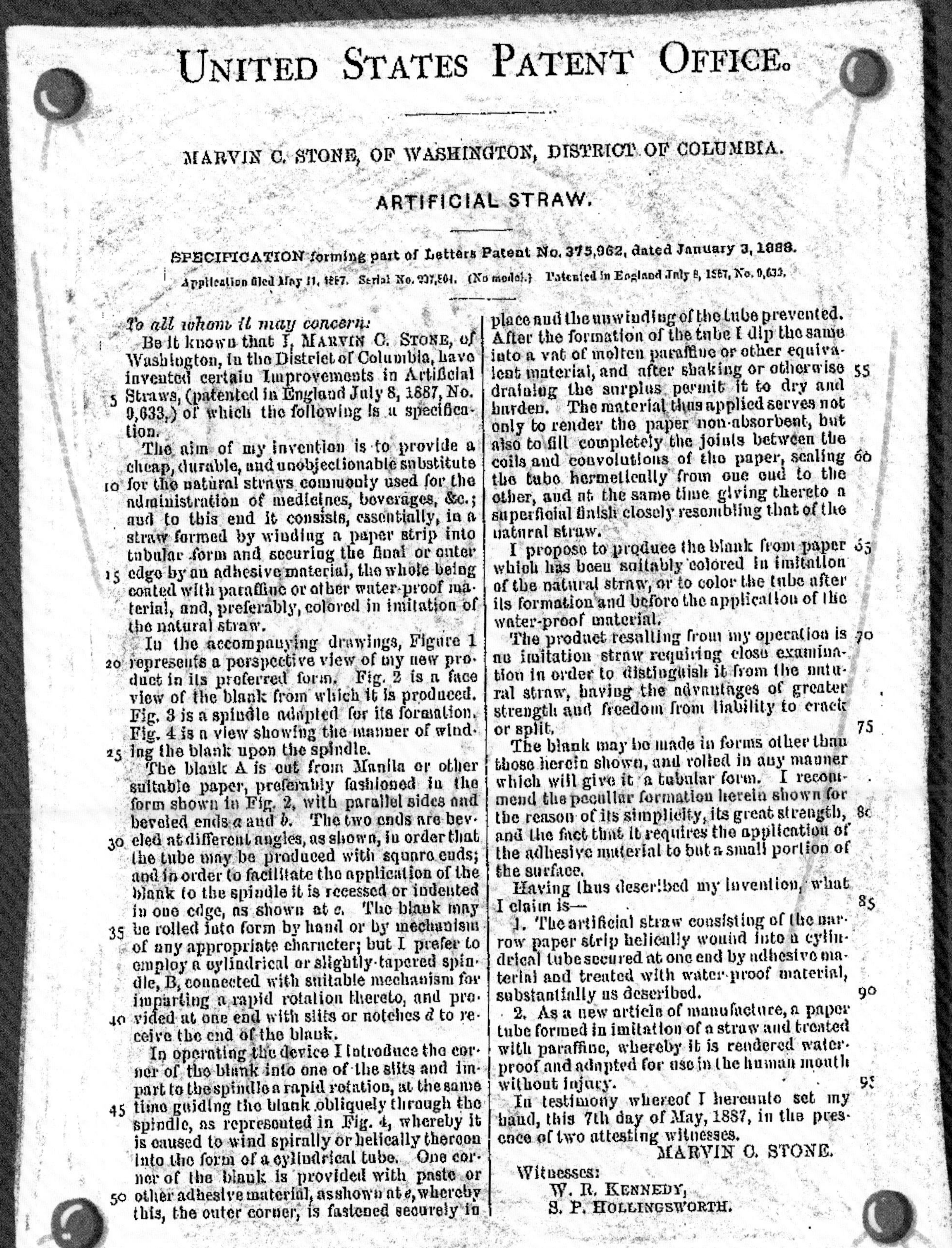

UNITED STATES PATENT OFFICE.

MARVIN C. STONE, OF WASHINGTON, DISTRICT OF COLUMBIA.

ARTIFICIAL STRAW.

SPECIFICATION forming part of Letters Patent No. 375,962, dated January 3, 1888.

Application filed May 11, 1887. Serial No. 237,504. (No model.) Patented in England July 8, 1887, No. 9,633.

To all whom it may concern:

Be it known that I, MARVIN C. STONE, of Washington, in the District of Columbia, have invented certain Improvements in Artificial Straws, (patented in England July 8, 1887, No. 9,633,) of which the following is a specification.

The aim of my invention is to provide a cheap, durable, and unobjectionable substitute for the natural straws commonly used for the administration of medicines, beverages, &c.; and to this end it consists, essentially, in a straw formed by winding a paper strip into tubular form and securing the final or outer edge by an adhesive material, the whole being coated with paraffine or other water-proof material, and, preferably, colored in imitation of the natural straw.

In the accompanying drawings, Figure 1 represents a perspective view of my new product in its preferred form. Fig. 2 is a face view of the blank from which it is produced. Fig. 3 is a spindle adapted for its formation. Fig. 4 is a view showing the manner of winding the blank upon the spindle.

The blank A is cut from Manila or other suitable paper, preferably fashioned in the form shown in Fig. 2, with parallel sides and beveled ends *a* and *b*. The two ends are beveled at different angles, as shown, in order that the tube may be produced with square ends; and in order to facilitate the application of the blank to the spindle it is recessed or indented in one edge, as shown at *c*. The blank may be rolled into form by hand or by mechanism of any appropriate character; but I prefer to employ a cylindrical or slightly-tapered spindle, B, connected with suitable mechanism for imparting a rapid rotation thereto, and provided at one end with slits or notches *d* to receive the end of the blank.

In operating the device I introduce the corner of the blank into one of the slits and impart to the spindle a rapid rotation, at the same time guiding the blank obliquely through the spindle, as represented in Fig. 4, whereby it is caused to wind spirally or helically thereon into the form of a cylindrical tube. One corner of the blank is provided with paste or other adhesive material, as shown at *e*, whereby this, the outer corner, is fastened securely in place and the unwinding of the tube prevented. After the formation of the tube I dip the same into a vat of molten paraffine or other equivalent material, and after shaking or otherwise draining the surplus permit it to dry and harden. The material thus applied serves not only to render the paper non-absorbent, but also to fill completely the joints between the coils and convolutions of the paper, sealing the tube hermetically from one end to the other, and at the same time giving thereto a superficial finish closely resembling that of the natural straw.

I propose to produce the blank from paper which has been suitably colored in imitation of the natural straw, or to color the tube after its formation and before the application of the water-proof material.

The product resulting from my operation is an imitation straw requiring close examination in order to distinguish it from the natural straw, having the advantages of greater strength and freedom from liability to crack or split.

The blank may be made in forms other than those herein shown, and rolled in any manner which will give it a tubular form. I recommend the peculiar formation herein shown for the reason of its simplicity, its great strength, and the fact that it requires the application of the adhesive material to but a small portion of the surface.

Having thus described my invention, what I claim is—

1. The artificial straw consisting of the narrow paper strip helically wound into a cylindrical tube secured at one end by adhesive material and treated with water-proof material, substantially as described.

2. As a new article of manufacture, a paper tube formed in imitation of a straw and treated with paraffine, whereby it is rendered waterproof and adapted for use in the human mouth without injury.

In testimony whereof I hereunto set my hand, this 7th day of May, 1887, in the presence of two attesting witnesses.

MARVIN C. STONE.

Witnesses:
W. R. KENNEDY,
S. P. HOLLINGSWORTH.

Straws became even more popular because of soda fountains and pop bottles.

Forty years went by before someone did something about the *next* problem.

Not everyone could reach the top of a straight straw.

Inventor Joseph Friedman was at the Varsity Sweet Shop in San Francisco with his daughter, Judith. She was having a milkshake but was struggling to reach the top of the straw to drink it.

Joseph put a screw inside a paper straw and wrapped dental floss along the grooves of the screw. This created ridges that allowed the straw to flex. Hello, bendy straw!

He received his patent for the "Drinking Tube" in 1937, but World War II was being fought at the time, so bendy straws didn't hit the market until ten years later.

His first sales were to hospitals that used the bendy straw for patients lying in bed.

About another ten years went by before someone did something about the *next* problem.

The paper straw sometimes ripped.

Plus, when the war ended, companies didn't need to make plastics for war materials anymore. They wanted to make different kinds of goods.

Companies started producing plastic products, including plastic straws. They were cheaper and more durable than paper straws.

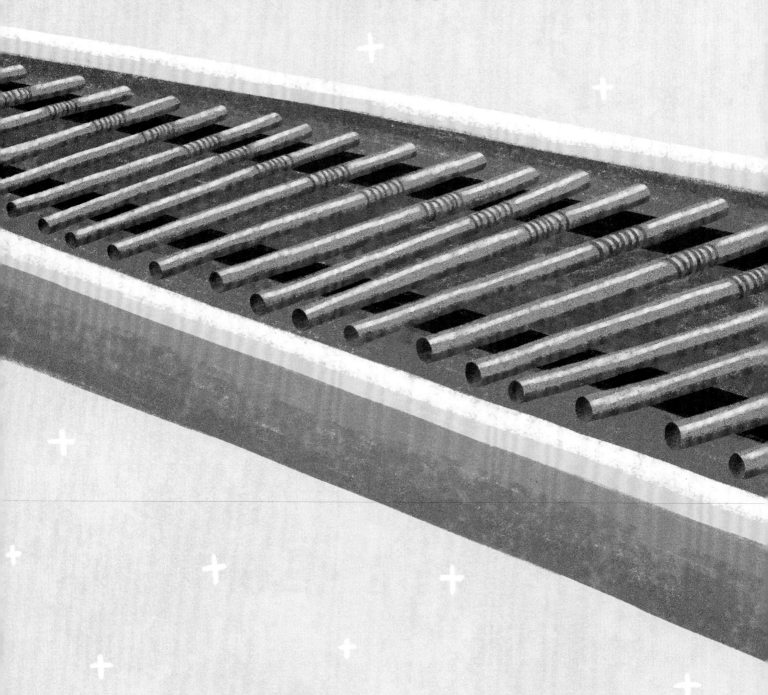

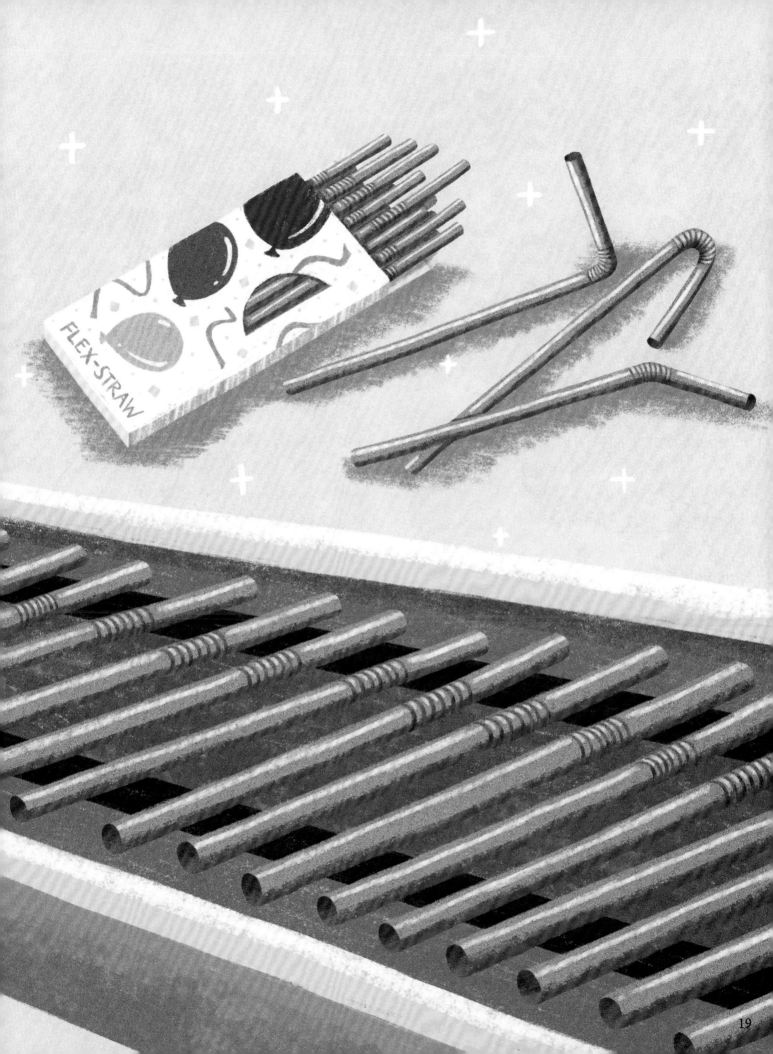

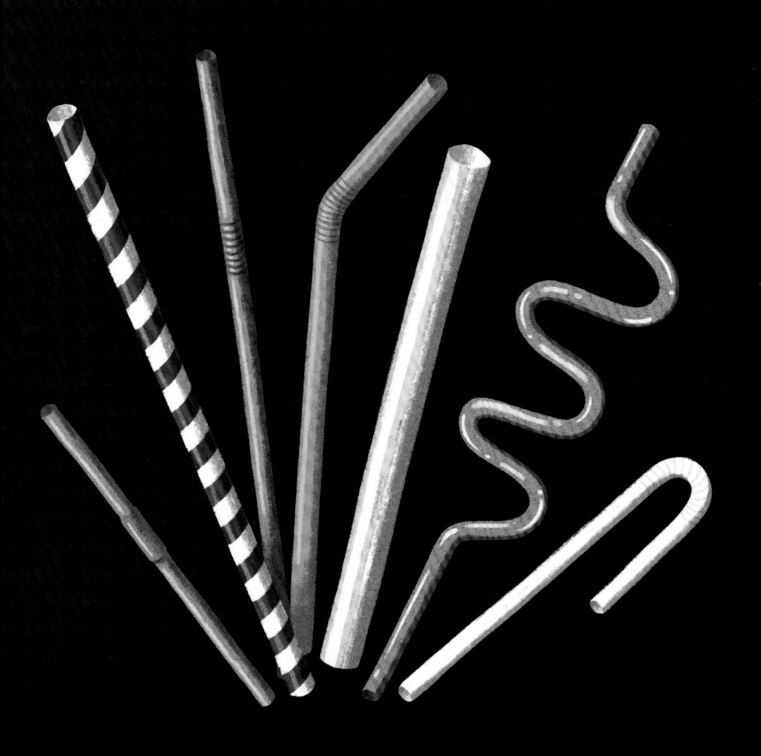

By the 1960s, plastic straws were everywhere.

But sometimes the solution to one thing *becomes* the problem . . .

No one planned for the effect these plastics would have on the environment.

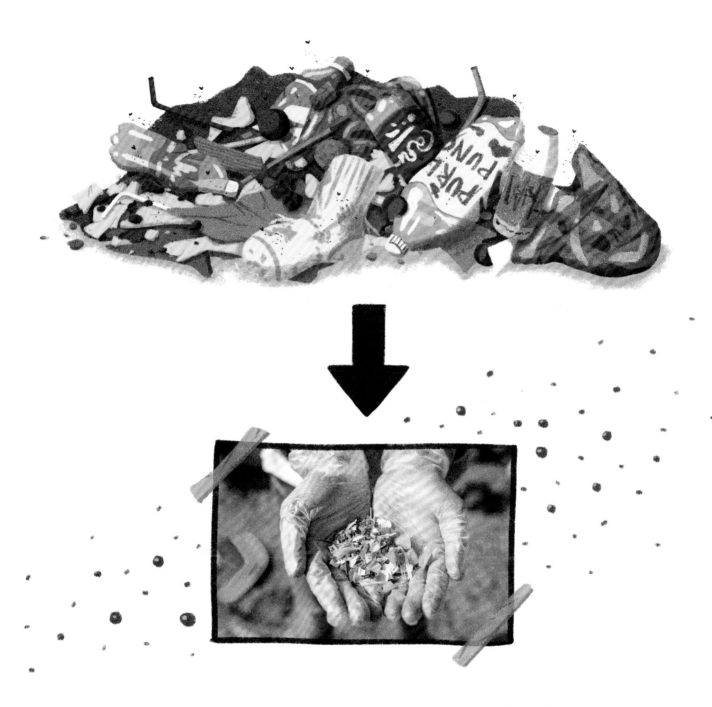

Single-use plastics are plastics that are used once and then thrown away, like water bottles, plastic bags, and straws. While they're useful and strong, they're not biodegradable, so they don't break down into the earth or dissolve in water. Instead, they break down into tiny little pieces called microplastics that are sometimes too small to even be seen. And they stay around forever.

Now that's an awfully long time for something that's only used once.

These plastics pollute our oceans and endanger sea life. Fish and sea birds ingest them by accident and also mistake them for food. Straws can get stuck in the airways of marine animals.

Because straws are so light, they can easily be carried by wind and water currents to other locations. Scientists have estimated that up to 8.3 billion plastic straws can be found on beaches around the world.

So, what is the solution?

The first step is realizing that everything we do matters, and that changing our habits can make a huge difference.

In 2011, a nine-year-old boy named Milo Cress began the "Be Straw Free" campaign after noticing how straws were often wasted. He spoke to straw manufacturers and estimated that 500 million straws are thrown out every day in the United States alone! That's enough to fill 46,400 school buses per year!

Many companies and organizations including restaurants, airlines, zoos, and aquariums all over the world are switching to paper straws or other biodegradable options. Some governments are banning plastic straws, or enacting restrictions like requiring restaurants to give straws only if a customer asks for one. Some are pledging to completely do away with single-use plastics. Organizations around the globe are working to clean up our oceans and waterways.

AQUARIUM ≈

BAMBOO STRAW

PAPER STRAW

METAL STRAW

Some people do use plastic straws for medical reasons. They need the straw to bend, and if a paper straw breaks apart, it could be a choking hazard. So until an alternative material is found, we should be mindful of their needs.

You can be part of the solution!

When you go to a restaurant, say "No straws please."
Drink from a cup.
Use paper straws.
Use reusable straws like stainless steel, bamboo, or silicone.
Share what you've learned.

Straws are only a portion of the plastics we use, but making good choices to protect our environment is an important start. Taking small actions can lead to bigger efforts and much-needed discussions.

We can choose our planet over plastic.
We can demand change.
And we can each start by saying, "That's the last (plastic) straw for me!"

AUTHOR'S NOTE

"From knowing comes caring, and from caring comes change."
—Craig Leeson, *A Plastic Ocean*

This book is about the straw, but it's important to note that plastic straws are only part of a growing issue. Single-use plastics come in many forms, including plastic bags, food containers, and water bottles. While plastics help us in a lot of ways, they are also polluting our oceans and filling up our landfills. Being aware of the problem and changing our habits are steps toward a solution. From there we can begin to demand change.

Two animals that have been affected by the plastic problem have helped start this revolution. In 2015, a video went viral of a plastic straw being pulled out of a sea turtle's nose. The Laysan albatross that inhabits the islands of Midway Atoll in the Pacific Ocean skims the surface of the ocean for food. Pictures show these birds with stomachs full of plastic.

Since plastic straws are something that most of us can easily do without, many groups have started there. It's a reminder that we can all make a difference.

The following organizations are working to make the switch from plastic straws to earth-friendly solutions. Check them out for more information.

Be Straw Free	http://ecocycle.org/bestrawfree
The Last Plastic Straw	https://thelastplasticstraw.org/
Strawfree.org	https://strawfree.org/

Parents and kids are also working to make the switch at their schools. You can let your voice be heard in your community as well. Get a group together to make a plan and pledge to stop using plastic straws. Ask local restaurants to make the switch to paper straws or to only give straws if customers request them. Reach out to companies and tell them you want eco-friendly products and packaging. Adults can contact their representatives to let them know they want change.

Take simple steps each day to help keep our earth healthy.

REFUSE. REDUCE. REUSE. RECYCLE.

National Geographic reminds us that "Every action matters."

SOURCES

Borenstein, Seth. "Science Says: Amount of Straws, Plastic Pollution Is Huge." *Phys.org*, Phys.org, 21 Apr. 2018, phys.org/news/2018-04-science-amount-straws-plastic-pollution.html.

Broda-Bahm, Chris. "The Straight Truth About the Flexible Drinking Straw." *Lemelson Center for the Study of Invention and Innovation*, Smithsonian Institution, 1 June 2002, invention.si.edu/straight-truth-about-flexible-drinking-straw.

Cress, Milo. "Be Straw Free Campaign." *Eco-Cycle*, 2016, www.ecocycle.org/bestrawfree.

Friedman, J.B. *Drinking Tube*. 28 Sept. 1937. U.S. Patent 2,094,268.

Gibbens, Sarah. "A Brief History of How Plastic Straws Took Over the World." *National Geographic*, 2 Jan. 2019, www.nationalgeographic.com/environment/2018/07/news-plastic-drinking-straw-history-ban/.

"Imitation Paper Straws." *The Lafayette Advertiser*, 8 June 1889, p. 6.

Joseph B. Friedman Papers, 1915-2000, Archives Center, National Museum of American History.

Stone, Marvin C. *Artificial Straw*. 3 Jan. 1888. U.S. Patent 375,962.

"The Patent Centennial." *Scientific American*, vol. 64, no. 14, 1891, pp. 213–215. JSTOR, www.jstor.org/stable/26102884. Accessed 9 Sept. 2021.

Thompson, Derek. "The Amazing History and the Strange Invention of the Bendy Straw." *The Atlantic*, Atlantic Media Company, 22 Nov. 2011, www.theatlantic.com/business/archive/2011/11/the-amazing-history-and-the-strange-invention-of-the-bendy-straw/248923/.

Thorpe, George W. "From Soda Straws to Defense: It's Done in D.C." *The Washington Post*, 27 Aug. 1941, p. 12.

Wilson, Lawrence, editor. *Itinerary of the Seventh Ohio Volunteer Infantry, 1861-1864: With Roster, Portraits and Biographies*. The Neal Publishing Company, 1907.

To learn more about plastics and their effect on the environment . . .

ONLINE

Search "The Great Pacific Garbage Patch." Located between Hawaii and California, it is the biggest accumulation of plastic waste in the world.

BOOKS

Abbing, Michiel Roscam. *Plastic Soup: An Atlas of Ocean Pollution*. Island Press, 2019.

Burns, Loree Griffin. *Tracking Trash: Flotsam, Jetsam, and the Science of Ocean Motion*. Houghton Mifflin Company, 2007.

French, Jess. *What a Waste: Trash, Recycling, and Protecting Our Planet*. DK Publishing, 2019.

Hood, Susan; illustrated by Christiane Engel. *The Last Straw: Kids vs. Plastics.* HarperCollins Publishers, 2021.

Pincus, Meeg; illustrated by Lucy Semple. *Ocean Soup: A Recipe for You, Me, and a Cleaner Sea*. Sleeping Bear Press, 2021.

Poynter, Dougie. *Plastic Sucks!: How YOU Can Reduce Single-Use Plastic and Save Our Planet*. Macmillan Publishers, 2019.

DOCUMENTARIES

Angela Sun, director. *Plastic Paradise*. 2014.

Craig Leeson, director. *A Plastic Ocean*. 2017.

Linda Booker, director. *Straws*. 2017.

Microplastics Photo Credit: Page 21-Photo 148276799 © David Pereiras Villagra | Dreamstime.com

INDEX

animals, *22*

bamboo, *28*

beverage(s), *3*

bird(s), *22*

bombilla, *6*

bus(es), *25*

China, *6*

civilization, *3*

Cress, Milo, *25*

environment, *20, 29*

fish, *22*

floss, *16*

Friedman, Joseph, *15–17*

grass(y), *4, 10*

hospital(s), *17*

invention, *12*

microplastic, *21*

Midway Atoll, *30*

mint julep, *10*

ocean(s), *22, 26*

paper, *10, 16, 18, 26–28*

patent, *12, 17*

pencil, *10*

plant, *6*

plastic(s), *18–29*

plow, *3*

Queen Puabi, *4–5*

reed, *4*

rye, *8-10*

sailboat(s), *3*

San Francisco, *15*

scientist, *22*

screw, *16*

soda fountain, *14*

silicone, *28*

South America, *6*

steel, *28*

Stone, Marvin, *10–13*

Sumer, *3*

Sumerian(s), *3–4*

Ur, *4*

Varsity Sweet Shop, *15*

Washington, DC, *10*

wheel, *3*

World War II, *17*

writing, *3*